In the pages of this book, young children will recognise a wide variety of familiar scenes and objects.

Some have been grouped together under headings. Others have been placed to show opposites or contrasts.

Read the words together and talk about the pictures. Explore how the pictures relate to each other and to your child's own experience.

Cover illustration by Peter Stevenson

A catalogue record for this book is available from the British Library

This book was first published by Ladybird Books as *Picture word book 1*

Published by Ladybird Books Ltd   Loughborough
Leicestershire   UK
Ladybird Books Inc   Auburn   Maine   04210   USA

Printed in England

Illustrated by Joanna Willi

Ladybird Books

ear

nose

mouth

What colour is your hair?

What colour are your eyes?

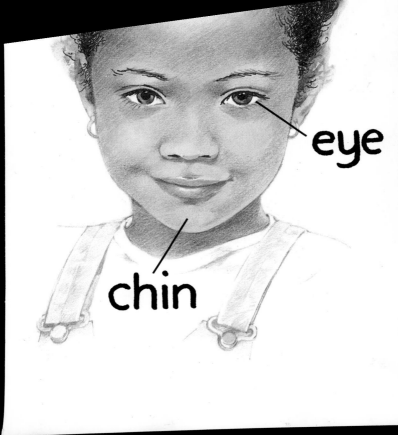

eye

chin

*Which of these do you think
will go fastest?*

Do you have a bicycle?

bicycle

motorbike

TOYS

teddy bear

ball

doll

What is your favourite toy?

cat

dog

plate

fork

knife

Can you lay the table?

glass

cup

saucer

spoon

brush

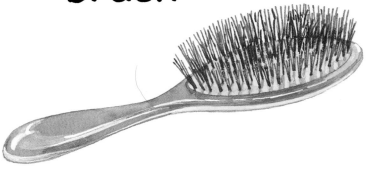

comb

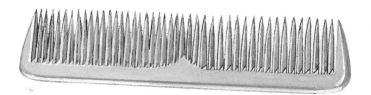

toothbrush

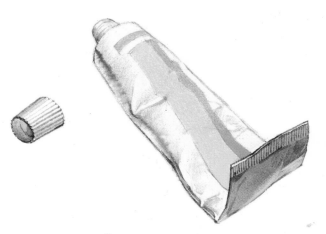

toothpaste

FRUIT

apple

orange

banana

grapes

telephone

television

What do you like to watch on television?

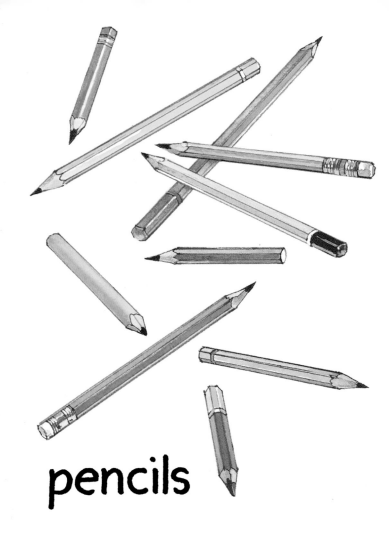

pencils

How many yellow pencils?

crayons

How many blue crayons?

table

chair

tap

toilet

bath

CLOTHES

jacket

trousers

sock

shoes

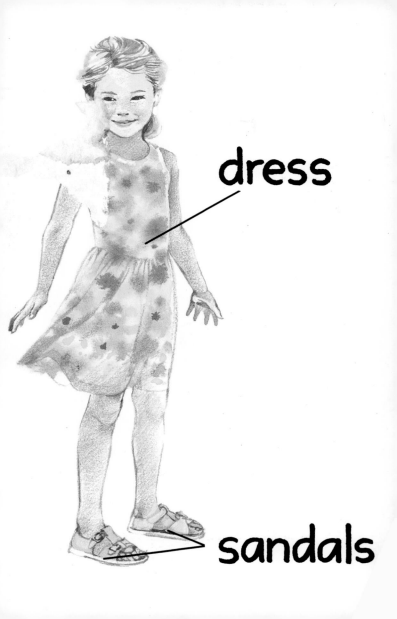

dress

sandals

sun

day

Talk about the differences between these two pictures.

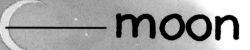

moon

night

Picture words in this book
(in alphabetical order)

apple	day
	dog
ball	doll
banana	dress
bath	
bicycle	ear
brush	eye
car	fork
cat	
chair	glass
chin	grapes
comb	
crayons	hair
cup	